AGAINST

THE

FORGETTING

Score composed by Hans Faverey, 1948.
Courtesy of Uitgeverij De Bezige Bij, Amsterdam

AGAINST THE FORGETTING

SELECTED POEMS

HANS FAVEREY

Translated from the Dutch and with a Foreword by
FRANCIS R. JONES

Preface by
ELIOT WEINBERGER

A NEW DIRECTIONS BOOK

Against the Forgetting is published by arrangement with Anvil Press
Poetry Ltd., Neptune house, 70 Royal Hill, London, England, SE10 8RT.

All poems were originally published in Dutch by Uitgeverij De Bezige
Bij, Amsterdam.

A version of the Foreword plus some of these poems first appeared in
Callaloo (Volume 21, No.3, Summer 1998).

New Directions gratefully acknowledges that the publication of this book
has been made possible with financial support from the Foundation for
the Production and Translation of Dutch Literature (www.nlpvf.nl).

Manufactured in the United States of America
New Directions Books are printed on acid-free paper.
First published as a New Directions Paperbook (NDP969) in 2004
Published simultaneously in Canada by Penguin Books Canada Limited

Library of Congress Cataloging-in-Publication Data

Faverey, Hans (1933-1990)
[Poems. English. Selections]
Against the forgetting : selected poems / Hans Faverey ; translated
from the Dutch and with a foreword by Francis R. Jones ; preface by
Eliot Weinberger.
    p. cm. -- (New Directions paperbook ; 969)
ISBN 0-8112-1555-5 (alk. paper)
I. Jones, Francis R., 1955- II. Title.
PT5881.16.A9A25 2004
839.31'164--dc22
                                        2003018021

New Directions Books are published for James Laughlin
by New Directions Publishing Corporation
80 Eighth Avenue, New York, NY 10011

CONTENTS

VI. from TROUBLESOME GODS (HINDERLIJKE GODEN), 1985

PREFACE

Aristotle: "[Thales] declared the first-principle to be water. . . heat itself is generated out of moisture. . . the seeds of everything have a moist nature."

Aristotle: "Thales conceived of the soul as somehow a motive power, since he said the magnetic stone has soul in it because it sets a piece of iron in motion."

Faverey: "All is born of moisture, / even life's heat. Lifeless / nature is animate too. / Proof: lodestone, // amber. Hence seed, / too, is always / moist in temperament."

Alcmaeon of Crotona: "Men perish because they cannot join the beginning with the end."

Outside of Holland almost no one has heard of Hans Faverey, for fate and his own predilections kept his work a secret abroad.

Heraclitus: "Nature loves to hide."

He wrote in a language not many speak and few foreigners now know. Boswell: "In the latter part of his life, in order to satisfy himself whether his mental faculties were impaired, [Johnson] resolved that he would try to learn a new language, and fixed upon the Low Dutch. . ."

He died in 1990 at age 56, at the moment when his national reputation might have propelled him onto the international circuit, which he probably would have avoided.

Faverey: "What hides beneath the / wordline, hides all but / in vain."

In Holland, despite prizes and acclaim, he tended to elude the gaze of the public eye. In his rare interviews, the answers were evasive.

Faverey: "Facts / consist of nothing."

He was born in Dutch Guiana, now Surinam, and moved to Amsterdam as a boy. His tropical childhood almost never enters the poems.

He worked as a clinical psychologist. Psychological insights, experiences, language, almost never enter the poems.

Democritus: "Man must learn that he is divorced from reality."

He met his wife on an island without vowels: Krk.

Friends have described their happy marriage, but in the poems the beloved is absent, remembered, the subject of a dream or a day-dream.

Faverey: "Memory is perception."

He played the harpsichord and wished he had composed more than a few occasional pieces.

He wrote series of short poems, and he wrote listening to Baroque fugues and variations.

Faverey: "in the repetition / shows the futility."

He called his poems "exercises in absence: detachment-exercises."

Faverey: "The utter emptiness / in every thing, which actually / is. . ."

Melissus: "What is empty is nothing, and what is nothing cannot be."

He loved the moment when a bouncing ping pong ball stops bouncing, but one doesn't know if it has finally come to rest.

Zeno: "If anything is moving, it must be moving either in the place in which it is or in the place in which it is not. However it cannot move in the place in which it is and it cannot move in the place in which it is not. Therefore movement is impossible."

He loved Zeno's arrow. His "Tortoise" is the one that outruns Achilles.

Melissus: "If Being were divided it would be in motion, and if it were in motion it would not be."

He titled a series "Sur Place," a psychological tactic from velo-drome racing: the cyclist remains on the side, motionless, feet on the pedals, and lets the opponents pass.

Faverey: "it works: the world stands still."

He shared the national obsession with still lifes, a term coined by the Dutch. Guy Davenport: ". . . *leven*, 'alive,' or drawings made from a model. A *vrouwenleven* was a female model, and one who, from time to time, while posing, needed to move; a *stilleven* – fruit, flowers, or fish – remained still."

Xenophanes: "God always abides in the selfsame place, not moving at all."

For Faverey, a still life is not only time arrested, but decay arrested. A still life is the opposite of a *nature morte*.

Still life: The subject of the individual painting is unchanging; the subjects of the genre are unchanging; the genre is unchanging. Absolute stillness. Davenport: "All the genres of painting except still life are discontinuous, and only the lyric poem, or song, can claim so ancient a part of our culture among the expressive arts."

Faverey: "I do not wish to know time."

His first book was called *Poems*; his second, *Poems II*. When asked how his work had changed over the years, he replied that the poems had gotten a little longer.

Faverey: "When there is nothing left / to do it for, / to do it with, // it stops of its own accord."

When asked if his later poems were more accessible, he replied: "I am better at it now."

Faverey: "Of course it's the principle that counts, // if there's a principle that counts."

Many of the poems have "it" for a subject, but it is difficult to know what "it" is.

All of his "homages" seem pitched to an opposite pole: the melancholic, melodramatic landscapes of Seghers; the perfect ricercars of Cavazzoni; the *Epic of Gilgamesh*; the delicate ornamentations of Couperin, composer of *The Bees, The Butterflies, The Voluptuous Lady, The Nightingale in Love.*

Heraclitus: "The hidden harmony is better than the obvious."

In all of his "homages," a glimpse of the coattails of his ostensible subject before it vanishes.

Faverey: "I have grown to love Sappho / since destruction / abridged her texts."

Among American poets, his company would have been George Oppen, William Bronk, Gustaf Sobin.

Like Oppen, free-floating, enigmatic, unforgettable lines. Like Oppen, *Poems* is his *Discrete Series*: contrary to most writers, the earliest work is the least loquacious, has the least connectives.

Oppen: "Closed car – closed in glass – / At the curb, / Unapplied and empty:" Faverey: "Standstill // under construction, demolition / Under construction. 'Emptiness, // So stately on her stem':"

Faverey: "As far as the eye can see, // the discrete has been seen."

Like Bronk, paradoxes in plain language, and lines that erase the preceding line.

Bronk: "We aren't even here but in a real here / elsewhere – a long way off." Faverey: "It is not yet now; // yet now has not just been."

Empedocles: "What is right may properly be uttered even twice."

Like Sobin, Mediterranean efflorescence – in Faverey, the Dalmatian coast – bursting through the seeming aridity of few words.

Sobin: "that the flowers aren't   ours, aren't / flowering for our voices. . ." Faverey: "What the vine wants // happens."

When asked what happens in his poems, he replied: "Things happen and at a certain moment they don't happen anymore. Finished, basta, the end."

Faverey: "He who cannot wait for the unhoped-for / will never hold out / until he cries: enough."

Against the Forgetting: "Oblivion knows no time."

ELIOT WEINBERGER

FOREWORD

HANS ANTONIUS FAVEREY was born in Paramaribo, the capital of Surinam (then Dutch Guiana), in 1933. In 1938 he moved to Amsterdam with his mother and brother. In 1953, while a student of psychology at the University of Amsterdam, he made the first of many visits to the Croatian coast. Here, on the island of Krk, he met his wife to be, the Croatian poet and comparative literature scholar Lela Zečković. Alongside his poetic work, he was a lecturer and consultant in clinical psychology at the University of Leiden. He died in Amsterdam in 1990.

Hans Faverey's first collection, *Gedichten (Poems)* of 1968, earned him the Amsterdam Poetry Prize. Though seen by some as "difficult" and "hermetic," the icily coherent, crystalline poems in *Gedichten* and in *Gedichten II*, which followed in 1972, were obviously the work of a rare poetic talent. The third volume, *Chrysanten, roeiers (Chrysanthemums, Rowers)* of 1977, however, which gained the Jan Campert Prize, met with undiluted praise. The poems are indeed more accessible, though they retain a sense of mystery and paradox. They are also slightly longer, setting a tone and format which he was to retain for the rest of his poetic life. Faverey's reputation was confirmed and strengthened by the volumes which followed: *Lichtval (Lightfall,* 1981), *Zijden kettingen (Silken Chains,* 1983), *Hinderlijke goden (Troublesome Gods,* 1985), *Tegen het vergeten (Against the Forgetting,* 1988). By the time of his last collection, *Het ontbrokene (Default,* 1990), Hans Faverey was generally recognized as the Netherlands' most eminent poet. Shortly before his death in 1990, he was awarded the prestigious Constantijn Huygens Prize for his whole oeuvre. In 2003, *Springvossen (Spring Foxes)* appeared, a posthumous collection of previously unpublished poems.

These are the biographical details. But what reflection do they have in his work? The answer is: precious little, at first glance anyway. Hans Faverey's poetry avoids easy messages and conventional forms. There are no simple landscapes or narratives, presented for their own picturesque sake or in order to mirror the poet's emotional state. As Faverey said in a 1988 interview: "You can't see from my poetry what I'm like in daily life." But he continued: "The autobiographical is in it piecemeal, is assembled on it or sneaks inside. Through associations, through ideas." And when we look closer, we can indeed sometimes see traces of his work as a clinical psychologist, for example, as in the poem "Now the hour is standing still," from *Chrysanthemums, Rowers*, prompted by his seeing the encephalogram of a dying man:

> Now the hour is standing still,
>
> everything breathes out parting,
> and stalls. This mouth or that
> still seems to be sucking
>
> at a tongue that is now scarcely able
> to do anything in return.

Faverey left Surinam while he was still a child; hence direct references to the Caribbean of his birth are few. Only in one cycle – "The Pond in the Lake" (from *Silken Chains*) – does Faverey, directly and movingly, address his Caribbean roots. Here he returns to Surinam, where his father is dying:

> In his house next to his house
> sits Spider; Son pays him a visit:
> they will never see each other again.
>
> 'You going to think of this land a lot' –

Spider, of course, is the resourceful Anansi of Caribbean legend, and his speech has Caribbean modulations (which I have tried to reproduce in translation): two clues that unlock the deep personal meaning of what might seem, on the surface, to be a coolly hermetic set of images.

This, however, seems at first sight overlaid by his passion for a European cultural heritage. Yet relatively few of his landscapes are recognizably Dutch. Unless, of course, one counts the many poems set in or alluding to his Amsterdam home, for the domestic interior has been a constant theme of Dutch art and literature ever since its 16th-17th century Golden Age. An exterior more frequent than that of the Netherlands is that of the Croatian islands, where he and Lela spent their summers, and which merges in turn into the timeless Aegean coastscapes of Homer and Sappho. Indeed, what is striking is the intellectual and geographical cosmopolitanism of Faverey's poetry – its very lack of regionalism or *couleur locale*. And this may be precisely where we hear an echo of his birthplace's creole culture, for all his landscapes are seen with the detached yet wondering eye of the migrant, the traveler. Even Holland – as in the poem "Chrysanthemums, Rowers", where waterways and fields become so indistinguishable that rowers seem to be rowing on land:

> ... Eight –
> rowing ever further inland;
> landscape, for there is
> no more water: overgrown
> landscape.

Experience and landscape, however, are no more than materials in Faverey's hands: they are not his subject matter. So what is? In a 1980 interview, he was asked whether there was a philosophy underlying his poetry. He answered: "The arrest of decay. The denial of movement. The search for the squared circle. In short, stopping time – in other words, the impossible." Like that of many poets, a key theme of Faverey's poetry is the transience of existence – the looming threat of death and silence (*zwijgen*: "not-speaking") that stalks us all. What makes his poetry unique is the solution he attempts: literally, to stop time.

One image Faverey uses is the paradox of Zeno's arrow. The shorter the slice of time, the less distance an arrow flies through the air; until, when the slice is infinitesimally thin, time stops still. In reality, however, time cannot be sliced infinitesimally thin: once the slices become thick enough to be perceptible, motion and change worm their way inside – a process we see happening in many of his poems.

Memory is another solution sometimes suggested to combat motion and decay – though if two events, repeated seemingly exactly, are never quite the same, how can the memory hope to reproduce the original event? In one poem, Hans and Lela revisit her aunt's garden in Croatia:

> as memory does with itself
> what it will, we begin
> biting once more, almost
> in unison, between
>
> the maize plants: she her
> apricot, I my apricot; ...

Another possible solution to the transience of the world is to distance oneself from it, by philosophy, or meditation with the aim of achieving nothingness. Philosophical means of attempting to break the bonds of time and the self are a frequent theme in Faverey's poetry. Analytic, linear thought processes cannot break free of "the net" of consciousness that ties us to the transient and the personal. Therefore the philosophical motifs that Faverey chooses are Eastern or pre-Socratic – the philosophy of paradox, not of logic; of non-self, not of self.

Faverey's poetry, then, is not a poetry of transparent representation, where words describe simple, coherent events or easily-recognized inner and outer landscapes. His is a poetry of association, of ideas linked by the discourse of paradox rather than by linear logic. He often uses language to give the illusion of representation, only, immediately afterwards, to deny that representation. If the depicted world is cancelled out, if what "hides beneath the wordline, hides all but in vain", then all we have left as the poem's theme is the word that depicts and cancels. This use of language not as a transparent window onto the world, but as subject in itself, is not merely a formal effect. It is also another way of distancing oneself from the world, from time, transience and decay: in other words, it is intimately linked with the content of Faverey's poetry.

To use language in this way, one must be its master. Hans

Faverey was famed in his lifetime for the perfection of his Dutch. His sentences are precisely sculpted, with every word, every nuance of grammar and punctuation carefully weighed. And every nuance of sound: though Faverey did not use conventional rhyme and rhythm, he did use structures of assonance. The resulting poetry, though sometimes hard to grasp with the conscious mind, gives a feeling of "rightness" at a deeper, intuitive level of perception, precisely through its beauty of sound and word-choice. And it is this mastery of the Dutch language which enables Faverey to push it beyond its limits, to where it becomes uncoupled from easily-graspable meaning – just as the best abstract artists, like Picasso, are those with excellent figurative skills.

All this, of course, presents the translator with a considerable challenge. This is particularly the case when Faverey focuses on the form of a word or phrase – by looking at the literal meaning of a Dutch idiom that may not exist in English, by breaking down a Dutch word's etymology that may not have a similar etymology in English, or by using puns, which almost never transfer across languages. Nevertheless, equivalents can sometimes be found – as in one poem, where the word *herberg* means both "inn" and "to shelter" or "to contain." Here I use the English word "lodge" in my translation:

In mijn aquarium huist hetzelfde aantal	My aquarium houses as many liters
liters water als daar wordt geherbergd.	of water as are lodged inside it.
Voor de herberg zit een oud man ...	Before the lodge an old man sits ...

It was also not always easy to capture the full richness of Faverey's complex sound-structures (as with the "h" and "t" sounds in the extract above), though it was usually possible to give a reasonable reproduction – except when other issues took priority, as with reproducing the pun on *herberg*, which is a key hinge between the two images in the poem above. The hardest, however, was to find convincing equivalents for language that breaks the rules. What the reader sees as a deliberate tactic in an original poem almost always looks like clumsy translation in a second-language version. The alternative, however – that of smoothing out any aberrations – loses a key element of what makes the poem special. Hence I always tried to keep the original's strangeness, even at the risk of being blamed for producing a version which may seem spiky and disconcerting.

Faverey, therefore, was a poet who used highly original techniques to tackle one of the oldest concerns of poetry, a concern that dates back to *Gilgamesh* and beyond: What is the nature of life and change, and how can one stop the slide into the void? The void took Hans Faverey tragically early – just as, too early or too late, it will swallow both you and me. But his words, words of a curious, puzzling beauty, still leak stubbornly through the silence.

●

When Anvil Press in London originally accepted an earlier version of this manuscript for publication in 1987, it ended with the cycle, "Against the Forgetting," which was all that had then appeared of the volume of the same name. Projected publishing dates became pushed back, as is their wont; meanwhile, more poems were published in Dutch and Hans's work began to acquire respect outside the Dutch-speaking world.

In late Spring 1990, as the metamorphosis from manuscript to book began in earnest, I heard rumors that Hans had been ill and began to realize why recent letters had gone unanswered. A phone call confirmed my worst fears. I went to Holland that weekend, arriving just in time to see the presentation of the Translators' Project at the Rotterdam Poetry International. A score of poets from every continent read their versions of poems from "The Parapet" and "Persephone, Resurrected"; Hans, unable to travel, read these two cycles on film – "more real than in the flesh," as he put it. When we talked together the following day, he showed me manuscripts which he was still editing and we agreed on poems that I should translate and add to the English collection while there was still time.

Two weeks later, only a couple of days after he had received the first bound copies of *Het ontbrokene*, Hans Faverey died. He was a cultured, considerate man, in both an intellectual and a personal sense. I remember the peace of his and Lela's book-lined Amsterdam flat just behind the Concertgebouw, Cabezón or Couperin open on the harpsichord, the quiet warmth of his voice, his shy wit. But perhaps the most enduring memory is of him reading his own poems, at festivals or – maybe indeed more real than in the flesh – filmed in his home, at the window by the ficus tree. The supreme master of written Dutch was also the consummate interpreter of his own verse: the key minor, the content – the beauty of a world surrounded by the ache of the void – lit by a tone just this side of sadness, the subtle modulations of syntax suddenly as transparent as crystal... When one hears Faverey read, one realizes as never before that, Zen-like, his is a poetry not only of words, but also of silences.

As he wrote his last book, Hans Faverey was all too aware that the silence lapping at all our words was about to extinguish his own. Perhaps the reader does not need this knowledge to appreciate these poems for what they are; but for me, and for all those who knew and loved him, it gives them an intenser poignancy.

•

In this New Directions edition, I have fully revised the translations from the Anvil edition. I have also added a number of poems, both from Hans Faverey's earlier volumes and from his exquisite posthumous collection, *Springvossen* (*Spring Foxes*), which appeared well after the Anvil selection. In so doing, I have tried to give the reader an impression of Hans Faverey's total oeuvre – as my tribute to an original and compelling poet, and also to a friend whose words still stubbornly leak through the silence which now surrounds him.

I would like to give my heartfelt thanks to Lela Zečković-Faverey for her painstaking help and advice at every level, from overall plan to individual word-choice; and to Hanneke Jones-Teuben and Willem van Toorn for their invaluable work in weeding out my mistakes and misinterpretations.

Francis R. Jones

AGAINST
THE
FORGETTING

I

from *Poems*
(*Gedichten*)
1968

*

Standstill

under construction, demolition
under construction. 'Emptiness,

so stately on her stem';
land in sight, blindfold.

*

No metaphor

intervenes here.
The match, in

accordance with orders,
communicated, burning.

*

The evacuated air-lock

(till someone's brains,
lungs, liver, spleen
no longer acknowledge him;

no longer have knowledge of him.)

*

A leak in the silence: noise –.

What codes? what filters?
(The 1st grape: splat!
The 2nd grape: splat!

The th-

*

So this man bows

to where nothing is;
picks up the rope,

rolls up the rope,
blows away the letters

and goes away himself.

*

The unbutterfly – the

grey, speckled one – was here.

One of the gifts: a gadget
for sucking the time

from things, from organisms.

The other gift
is best left unmentioned.

*

Dominance

of the clotted; insectoid
movements; selection tests

with semantic double filters –.
There is still communication,
but of the type that

bites its tail and drives its tail-
sting straight through its head.

II

from *Poems 2*
(*Gedichten 2*)
1972

Cycle for the Thin Girl 1

*

Shouldn't we be leaving here?

Everything's getting overexposed.
Here it already has a different name
and doesn't smell of much.

Or should we stay here.

Should you want to stay here.

*

Distance. What does distance matter;

how does distance work. Can it
even unwind a man,
then wind him up again?

Of course it's the principle that counts,

if there's a principle that counts.

*

What direction's it coming from?

The same direction. And are
the other data correct?
As far as one can tell.

What do you think you'll do now?

Whatever will you do now.

*

The end? No. Almost

the end? No. But
what do you mean by
no: – salt as well?

Can you hear me: salt as well?
Yes. Salt as well? Yes, salt.

*

Or should we stay here:

should I want to stay here.
When the upper lip is lifted
the teeth feel cold.

When both lips are gone,

your teeth feel colder still.

*

3 in the morning, 4 at night;

okay?). Parting from a series
of shapes; precisely what is silting up
inside you, you do not know.

Round skull, angular teeth.

Your *sun* won't shine long enough now.

*

Old rain; new rain.

Prendre la balle au bond
or missing it. Fur, from a fox's
armpit; stealing a clock,

and keeping your ears shut.

Dashing the egg against the stone.

*

(Can you still hear me?)

Say slowly after me: can
you still hear me? Words, dredged
through such powders: are they already

becoming glass? What a distance.
Say slowly after me: can y-

from *Cape Lava*

*

Pelican to the

north: signal. Crystal
families still whining:

signal. Swan blows into mouth
(come on) – signal. With whip-
and wingstrokes: as if light

is dawning in pumice,

in wolfsbane. No, sea doesn't
sound like that. No; that's not the sound

of sea. Come on – (Laughing: the way

she combed her hair): he's waiting. Does

the paper I trampled on crackle? can you

hear the sentence you speak? Come on,
my love. Don't worry about the details:
it's time. 'The boat grazes the bank.'

Come on: he's waiting.
Don't get personal: he *is* a

surly ferryman. Have you got the
money? Have I got the money?

(Come on). He's waiting; they are waiting.

Come on, my love – drain your glass.

III

from *Chrysanthemums, Rowers*
(Chrysanten, roeiers)
1977

from *Hommage à Hercules Seghers*

*

Emptying one's head

with one's hand on one's heart.
Hitting my forehead
to empty my heart.
Meanwhile, enticing distance,

as distance should
be: enticing.

So I can stay at least

a nose in front
of who I am becoming,
before I am winter
and am extinguished.

*

Nothing is wiped out as fast
as a butterfly fluttering down
shortly before an explosion.

With the same bang
as it bursts asunder,
it regains its balance.

A butterfly for a butterfly;
a text for a text;
a death for a death;

a bang or no bang;
a fluttering or
no fluttering.

*

When the time comes,
time fills with itself,
grows full of itself;

when time becomes one
of those spheres that slowly,
almost unnoticed,
pushes, presses itself

through itself;
and stone
kisses stone
and water drinks

water dry:
O absence –
most heartfelt.

*

I sit in my circle
and imagine an infinite
number of polygons:

I can see me doing it.
The boat, drawn up

on land, is no longer
mine, no longer needs
to be mine. I am
almost where I need to be:
even if I were sitting

on the shore myself, or
rather: lying on the shore,

beneath eared, white or
almond willows, where
the harps have long been
hanging; the strangled.

*

Smoke from the smokehole,
the hiss in the funnel,
your footprints, pursuing
themselves in the sand.

The ruins on the Euphrates,
or elsewhere. The columns
of Palmyra, or elsewhere.

Persisting in motion;
clinging to motion,
if it does not exist:
movement, motion.

The arrow is still.
The boat lies on the bank;
the spider will never empty
its fly. Not even a flea
can spring between
death and life.

from *Hommage à Sapho*

*

Now the hour is standing still,

everything breathes out parting,
and stalls. This mouth or that
still seems to be sucking

at a tongue that now is scarcely able
to do anything in return.
What is to be done? Is
standstill spreading at
impossible speed?

Are these still reeds waving there?

Or is all that still waves
the remains of language on a flickering
screen in a shrinking center?

*

Why? Because I am sitting
here, silence surrounding me
like the block of paraffin
wax I am sitting in,

or not sitting in: if this
is no block of paraffin wax,
but a featherweight foaming
awayness, where I
becomes elapsed in
during zenotalk,

and only the memory of
so much unsaid about nothing
keeps the crystals still intact.

*

He who cannot wait for the unhoped-for
will never hold out
until he cries: enough.

Each island keeps

the best book: itself.
The horse did not kick:

a blacksmith died.

I have grown to love Sappho
since destruction
abridged her texts.

from *Watch, Ship of the Desert*

*

Mir nix: dir nix.

Having no use for something.
Needing nothing from someone.
Has the sea left you speechless?
Has sea left her speechless?

Though the eyes you find beautiful
be almost of smokestone, the stone
that likes you goes up in smoke.

Having had no use for something.

Never having to go anywhere.
Unable to forget anything.
Making nothing of nothing.

Dir nix: mir nix.

*

Maybe only much later,
when word and springboard
have long since shrivelled,

and the bluebottle
is in full bloom –

greenish with memory
of blue, and reality
is slowly hauled to the surface:
a diving suit with someone

still in it; if you or I would
read this again: to know what
it says, it said, or is to come.

from *River Landscape with Bloodtime*

*

for Rein Bloem

Did this man here have
to lie down there in order
to let his blood run
free, and drain that
poppy to the final drop –

the plain, run dry as far

as the horizon; with the air
above all having smoothed
itself at last: the fore-
head of a blind man
peering into his distance.

*

Same old river landscape;
the flowers of alum; the lapping
monotonous; the ferryman, the dog,
the coin, the crossing;
the knife in the sacrificial beast

with the good or evil liver;

the blind ass in the mill;
the singing which is no longer
heard, the language which has
been forgotten; the vicious dog;
the body – just left there.

from *Hommage à François Couperin*

*

As far as the eye can see,

the discrete has been seen.
In how far am I thought,
if I conclude that I

can never have existed?
He who lies blows away;

words mean nothing.
He who speaks the truth
is a Cretan too.

*

In seed and crystal
always the same

vanishing point –
one fine day
it is night: a
put-up job.

What hides beneath the
wordline, hides all but
in vain. The scorpion

does not stir when I
lift the stone. There is
no scorpion anyway;
let alone someone

lifting a stone
no longer a stone.

from *Touched*

First the message kills
the receiver, then
it kills the sender.
It does not matter
in what language.

I stand up, throw
the balcony doors open
and take a breath.

The gulls circling
above the snowless street
I will not entice
with gestures of feeding.

I light a cigarette;
return to my post,
and take a breath.

There is nothing to dream.
Everything is possible.
Little matters.

Chrysanthemums, Rowers

*

The chrysanthemums
which are in the vase on the table
by the window: these

are not the chrysanthemums
which are by the window
on the table
in the vase.

The wind which is bothering you
and making a mess of your hair, this

is the wind which is messing up your hair;
it is the wind you no longer
want to be bothered by
when your hair is in a mess.

*

Only when someone in a photo
stands as large as life
waiting for his death
is he recognized.

They are all standing on the bank,
watching their own birdie;
laughing: all of them.

No one recognizes himself in this photo.
What does suddenly mean in a mirror?
Mirrors never recognize anyone.
What does suddenly mean in a photo?

If soon I can see a hand in front
of my face, let me hope
it is a hand of my own
or it is a hand
which wants to belong to me.

*

If I want to do something,
should I have already got up
to want to do it; or should I
have wanted to have already

done it: to be able
to get up in such a way

that I would have had to do it;

and in so doing
the thread being lost,
did as it wanted itself
done, sans rancune:
though nothing had happened,

and I did not wish myself absent,
for I did not know myself that way,
as it was about to happen.

*

If it brings anything about,
and has forgotten itself,
it is in vain
and for God's sake.

The utter emptiness
in every thing, which actually
is, and as such is active,
and merges with the echo
of the last word

(that now refuses to pass
the lips); which first care-

sses lips, only to eat them away
without hesitation: this hopeless lack,
which ties knots everywhere in water
and is a needle in bread.

*

Little by little –
they are drawing nearer: 8 rowers,
growing ever further inland

in their mythology:
with each stroke ever further
from home, rowing with all their might;
growing till all the water is gone,
and they fill the whole landscape

to the brim. Eight –
rowing ever further inland;
landscape, for there is
no more water: overgrown
landscape. Landscape,
rowing ever further

inland; land
without rowers; over-
rown land.

IV

from *Lightfall*
(*Lichtval*)
1981

from *The Tortoise*

Flash of darkening;

I know it is here:
like this, as it has become

itself. Not my sleep,
nor my waking;
not my words.

Here it is:

examining itself; spinning
on its axis, never letting up.
So engrossed in its game
that it has forgotten itself

in a droning gadfly, the
horsefly I now have to kill

before it stings me.

*

I have forgotten what I

was supposed to do here.
So here I stayed.
Of all the things

which can be done,
and are going to do themselves,
I still ought to be able
to manage one now and again:

one of those greengauze, motionless

dragonflies; a backwards-swimming
fish. A circus artiste, fallen
from her ball, stepping back
at once – That's it:

there she stands: she spreads her arms,
her legs are slim. I breathe again;

it works: the world stands still.

Exorcism

'You're making me into something I'm not.'

Then she had to stoop

to pick something up; I saw
a few vertebrae,
then quickly touched

her spine.

She shivered; turned,
stood up straight;
greets me with a laugh

and is gone.

*

Having been lying on one's left side;

having to lie on my right side.

The unforgettable face:
remembered with ever

greater effort, seen

again. In it, the eyes;
the cheekbones,
the nose; her mouth

which I never knew.

*

That you never existed.

I suddenly let myself slip;
and I hide my face.

The winter is long dead.

The swifts are back.

Have I always loved you;
or has she never existed.
Memories
are not memories.

Memory is perception.

*

Where she now is, now

I do not know. Just as she

happens to think of me, I
might happen not to think of
her. So, precisely when there is

nothing, there is always

something. By denying
motion I cannot even
manage it here,

manage it now.

*

As soon as it looks at itself

it is never anything else.
It is indivisible,
innumerable.

Come and stand on my shoes again:
then I can see your face.

It is broad daylight;
it has rained;
your eyes are glistening for something;

an ant is searching for something.

*

It's clearer now in my head;
I think I am in my head;

I can see the other islands
again. The sea appears
to have calmed down as well.

And so I repeat myself:

controlled despair about nothing.

The myrtle has started to blossom again.
With a fresh laurel branch
I manage to beat off
most of the flies.

*

She stoops

to pick something up:
because she had dropped something.

To see her stoop like that

I got her to drop something.
Before she leaves the room
and closes me behind her,

I get her to do it one more time.

And that's enough: no more.
At last: off you go.

Farewell.

from *View of Rhenen*

*

Lightfall:
couched with reasons,
the standstill opens
of something else than

housed in this blade, glinting

as it is, not yet tempted

and seduced by blood,
as if it were all a vision
already unsure of itself,
reduced in view of itself
to its source.

Murmur, preceding
the murmuring.

The self-opened mouth,

closed with its mouthful of sand.
Strange there's no beach here;

that the beach isn't here where

I am. The self-dying, even
during dilation. Such a short-
lived ever having shivered,
frozen in a blink of its eye;

the self-

begetting, self-
uplifting lethal.

*

Behind the light, deeds are dead.

Once night falls
were asters ever.

While the tomcat rises

as if to leave, an oyster
opens or closes,
the thornback, pregnant,
approaches the shore,

the fishhook, her net.

*

So is it a dream after all;
and the dream
itself a dream as well:

a promise which is kept,

as when I live up to myself,
on top of myself, falling
downstairs, forgetting in my haste
the missing steps, keeping, even

now, to the same rules

at the bottom of the stairs, lost
down there in the desert sands.

It won't be long now before

one of those prophetic
memories breaks from its seed:
a ford in the river

for one to ford oneself. And
me seeing, again and again,
one of those mules, with
its bales of sodden purple wool,

brace itself and climb

the bank, while the water
still gushes out of the wool.

*

Or, by lingering,

by holding back and
by staying here, did

the forgottenlike arise as if

by itself: the forever retreating,
self-retaking, deathfar fleeting;
as if someone or other,
leaning back, immobile,

in his bath of smoke and salt,

had become one with the
current, the riverbed, the course.

*

Open, unrecognizable.

The self-tormenter
is no longer tormented.
It is time: with a jerk
the curtain opens:

das Jenseits – view of Rhenen,

the other bank. The dagger which
no longer knows itself; the swan's
neck retracted between poppies. But
later, in my own time, one of those
big black crows, approaching from the
mainland, flying above the same sea

which still roars on in the shell,
here, in the palm of my hand.

from *Lightfall*

Where the apricot tree
stood still then
I stand still now.

Between the gladioli
I know the spot
where she stood then:
she threw me the apricot –
then. Now,

as memory does with itself
what it will, we begin
biting once more, almost
in unison, between

the maize plants: she her
apricot, I my apricot;

while the little foxes still prowl
through the vineyard, and the sea,
whispering: she is not with me;
no, you will not find it here;
she is not in me.

from *Sur place*

It is snowing

but is no longer snowing.
When it started to snow
I went to the window;

I went missing.

Sometime then,

just before the snow started
falling again, into great,
ever slower flakes,
it must also have

stopped snowing.

*

This is the penalty:

how nowhere I am.
The wave which dived through me
has filled my ears:
I cannot see a thing.

Whatever I may do,

nothing is added,

nothing missed. Sometimes
a board creaked in the floor;
or a vine tendril brushed
a stone in the wall
surrounding the vineyard.

*

When there is nothing left
to do it for,
to do it with,

it stops of its own accord.
The fingers leave their hand

and drop their hands. The feet
are free – bite the dust
one by one. Whatever still

lies there is suspended, word
by word. Only the wind

still blows, till
it runs out too,
wherever it will.

*

Oblivion knows no time.

Water would not know time,
nor does the circle know time;
I do not wish to know time.

So, in the end, even Mohammed

is forever leaving the same tent:
moving towards his mountain
together with the shadow that
is becoming his peacock; hesitant,
almost hesitating – Just as

a mountain looks seaward

through its sieve,
to see its fall
before evening comes,

and does not care.

V

from *Silken Chains*
(*Zijden kettingen*)
1983

Girolamo Cavazzoni, who disappeared in context

*

If only I were who I have remained.
If only nothing arose from the same.
And that standstill would break free
from the word which conceals it:

to infuse the blanching
absence creeping up
to my knees,

which wants to be rid of me
as soon as I no
longer speak.

*

Forcing into oneself and
forcing through oneself: parting,
seeking rest in what is left
when breath and its object

cancel one another out;

and all the water in the sea,
washing against the shore of the sea,
washes back into itself, each
generation of leaves falling
back once more, towards
the abyss, the orchard.

*

The summer has grown old
with the shadow of its fish

and the burning wheel on
yonder hill has stopped
burning. Above the rocks
a bird of prey is circling

and drawing closer.

Standing at the bow, I cast
anchor between the brambles,
turn round once more,
and leave the terrace.

*

Lisping of sometimes silken chains,
which in the foaming, however
scarcely, seem always

to have been shifting –

So that the vase, where blossoms
unforgivable smoke in honor
of smoke, now be nothing more
than a persistent drift into
dispersion, in that the light

still recognizes itself
as recollection.

*

A ball is at rest, or it is,
moving, in search of rest.

The mirror, filled to the brim
with what occurs, repeats itself
ex improviso: semblance and essence
recover each other's balance.
The god I name and do not name

seems to yield and not
to want to yield.

The afternoon prophesies nothing
else than itself. The brass box
on the windowsill now holds everything,
but nothing most of all. The keyboard,
however, ever more fiercely present,
now keeps a more melodious silence.

The Ordered

*

The earth, being earthwork.
That I am on earth, howsoever,
to draw breath: beneath the firm-
ament over us, overall.

The earth and its rivers;
her rivers. Now and again a

river goes underground, holing
up for a while in caves.
Some rivers end in sand.
The earth as worthy of mention.
The world as quicksand.

*

What is of fire falls to no other share.
However the existent holds fast:
it falls foul of fire. And where
there is fire, there is smoke:

voices smothered in smoke.
The world as a tuning-fork

made up of smoke. The boat
glides by, in it, smoldering,
the fiery wheel. Gloaming: each
spark finds its fire, each apple
its flesh.

*

Default of wind.

Salt crystal, from which a storm
is driven. Ant, into whom an ant
is blown, till death
follows – fulfillment.

Coolness: the world as survivor,
as memory of perfection,

coolness, of absence, of here.

How beautiful you are sitting there,
just before you begin to speak,
still having displaced no air,
your hands still in your lap.

*

The same riverbank, mine:
far and wide everything applying
to itself. A riverbank is
an armpit, also known as eyebrow,

or arrowdew, swiftsnow.

The day is short, the night is short.
The eternal coughing; the voiceless

whisper. The deadly flag
which propagates the earth.
This is your fire, this your breath.
The world as representation:
addresses crumbling to dust.

from *The Net*

*

Captured in his own net:
where is my octopus, fox
of the sea-dwellers?

Withdrawing into his maze,
the fox ponders, the flushed
admired: system once
compared to eight feet.

The hunter who kills them

is speedier, gaudier,
fickler than the back
of a snake which light
delights in.

An angler fish does nothing other
than is done by me with the muse,
once things have reached this pass.

All is born of moisture,
even life's heat. Lifeless
nature is animate too.
Proof: lodestone,

amber. Hence seed,
too, is always
moist in temperament.

*

Changing fortunes of war: eclipse
of the sun. Looking at the stars
and not seeing what's in front
of your feet. And now
Pythagoras

won't let me eat beans.

Or that I am dealt a solemn
blow if I nod off: caught out,

captivated with my own net. It
is myself, anyway: the hunter
flushing me out in order
to merge with me.

*

The same net, hung out to dry,
redyed. Beyond the horizon
there hides a new horizon
beyond which hangs drying

the sort of fishing net meant.

Now what else is there left
to do? I need to shake myself free
from myself. To be able once again
to cast the net as one should.

The Pond in the Lake

*

for A. T. Faverey (1905–1981)

The pond lies inside the lake
and beckons. If I'm sitting in my room
and I want to hear leaves,
I have to think of poplars,
or go hear poplars

where they are.

Have I ever heard
a chestnut-leaf fall in my head?
Or did I ever fall there
headlong into a pond?

*

The chestnut is eating out of my palm;
I sit with my face
to the wall I'm bleeding from.
If I so much as move a muscle
I have to admit I'm

a shellfish. I flutter

my wings until they're dry,
till they've evaporated. The feared
draws near: the feigning begins.
I have dismissed too little.

*

Inside the palm-nut lies a fish
which I am not. If I run back
to the lake, giving it all
I've got, I will have forgotten
who and what I had to kill,

to sacrifice in myself:

the first victim first, or first
the second victim. By refer-
ring to my self I lose
what I'd wanted to harbor.

*

On the strength of what's no longer here
I try my best to rake it back;
never wish to tire of seeing, even now,
your mouth which without your face
serves no purpose any more.

Inside the lake

lies the pond, ready and waiting.
Just because I was there
when they were passing by,
those hummingbirds are playing
havoc in my head.

*

So I start up anew as of old.
Splendid black ice, I cried,
you could skate here. Yet
the same image was no longer
a beginning. Still, even now,

you have only to wish it

and you can shake your hair so
that the walls of the nameable
come tumbling down and the open plains,
beyond the sound-stream, are hacked

*

down, till nothing remains of
what you were dreaming of.
How beautiful you are: almost coming
from you, I became that once.
I sit inside my pond

and ford the river which
swears me to silence.

Some forms are fordable;
others are not, or less so.
A pound of lead equals a pound
of feathers. It hardly ever helps

*

if grief, as foreseen, comes to a dead
end. In his house next to his house
sits Spider; Son pays him a visit:
they will never see each other again.

'You going to think of this country a lot' –

he stresses this,
adjourning death –

'You never going to forget it.'
The same little hollow vanishes
as soon as I open my fist:
I have never existed either.

*

In one of those early evenings
which are so rich in themselves,
he became passed away. The yearning
which had known itself within him
till then, went out. She who was
with him, roused him out of shrouding

or worries about a text

which I must leave unspoken here.

'*What* did you say?' he asked, as if in-
sisting on repetition. She, however,
repeated the message, at which he
understood and died just like that.

from *My Little Finger*

What happens when, in the depths
of the night, all the lights
burning, every thing

confirms its presence,

and rises as summoned

up to its base;
nor do I, once I have
taken me into myself,
know what is to be done, nor
what is to be left undone.

*

What gives rise to the certainty
of renouncing all that is salvaged,
even beneath a waning moon,
has proved so far to be nothing.

Even less gives me a sense

of what has consisted of nothing
so far. Even the waxing moon
rules out salvation: lapsed
certainty; unravelled existence.

*

Now it is here;

now it is not-here.
How is thrusts through itself
takes place between not yet

and nevermore. Once under

way, it moves neither where
it is, nor where it is not.
Given free rein
it keeps slipping from who
stands fast: now from one,

now from another. And how someone

can turn away and never
come back; stumbling;
a shivering for good.

*

Now I, walking backwards,
keep throwing these pebbles one

by one over my left shoulder,

and even the mist's downiest plumage
is becoming homeless too, what happens
is that – just as the corn had once
begun to blow, and I, grown reckless,
doused myself in the rye –

cleansed, second by second

sucks me through itself,
as if the roar of the sea, though
far away, were already aware of me,
had already detached itself to me,
long before I ever come to be.

*

It is not yet now;

yet now has not just been.

They are not the same leaves which
are casting themselves in their laps:
it is the river being reminded
of the river flowing here.

To be able to prove it,

to be man enough to do so,
the time is now ripe:
even if it fails.

*

Inhospitable facts no longer serving
a purpose; these have made me

what I have become:

these I hold in honor. Facts
consist of nothing. A pool
of clear water holds most
thoughts of absence.

But still I come running with two

hands full of water: here –
God is great, but no greater
than his failure. Any word
would rather swallow itself than
have to learn to swim like this.

*

When: what you see is there no more;
even the same river is there no more;
Pan holds back his cry, no nymph or
non-nymph cuts the waterline;

smoke inhales itself, blood
hides from blood

in a blood-slit – dagger

whose hand has fallen away;
hand raised to raze itself –
only then is there sense in stripping
the sentence of all its words.

from *Unhomely Glow-Worm*

*

An early evening as it should be.
Inside it is no less pleasant
than outside. I'm thinking of little,

of nothing in particular.

It is becoming now again. It is now almost
no longer early evening. It will shortly

be dark: then I'll switch my desk lamp
on. Been and gone – fourteen days
beyond the longest day. Still enough
plain paper. Later I'll get
drunk than sooner.

*

Ever more of the same;
nevermore the same one as then.
It once arose as if of its own
accord, now casting itself
back, now forth;

caught itself up, forsook itself
in nothing, forecast itself,
casting itself back and forth,

as if it were nothing. And nothing

it was, nor would it ever
have been so, had I not been so
sure of the unchange-
able being-so of things.

*

Nothing comes to be
which has not once been so away
before washing ashore: as

love lets itself wash ashore,

sometimes shell-less;

out of eyesight;
long gone in one ear
and out of the other.

I rattle my glow-worm
in its jamjar. I am left
with the dark; after that
I become the same for good.

from *To Ningal*

What the west wind left her with.
How she takes pity on what has
outstripped her. By means

of her mirror she smashes a pane
of glass. By forgetting her
I discover nothing else.

I hit two flints together:
misfire. Once out in the street
I stand still. Does she love me?

*

How is nothings itself
totally eludes me.

The sky, so clear and just as black,

has cast anchor in its sea;
reiterates something which still
remains escaped. The void on horseback;
the snail on the razor.

One by one I drop away, and become
what takes possession of me: calls me,
and was called by me.

*

Following the river upstream.
Many willows, many stones; the rush
of rapids. And reeds, which
in the language of this place
sound as they are: reeds
in a gentle breeze.

An old woman, singing out loud:

to herself, amid
her surroundings.

A brief greeting, a cough. Then
the singing is resumed, louder
now, it seems. I only catch sight of them
a little further: both her cows,
beside the water.

from *Thresholds*

*

Only when all has been ordered
and every thing has taken place

does chaos come to light.

A wind blows up which rises
to a storm and is mentioned nowhere
in the books now closing,

almost oysters.

*

Something like a desert of his own:
of this, man is made: uniform
rose, on a uniform footing,

leached bare – in order to withdraw

from the dream into the light that
comprises him; that without him
will no longer let itself fall
on the skin he now must wear.

*

My aquarium houses as many liters
of water as are lodged inside it.
Before the lodge an old man sits,
upright, elbows on the table
before him, his hands half-folded,

seeing into the valley.

In open fields there stands a tree
that is an oak, left standing
to shadow what is at hand.
Grasses; animals. Never dissolving
in himself, self-outcasting: man.

*

Why is it like this; and when
will it stop being so?
One glance through opened eyes
and the door slams shut.

The prisoner of his imagination

is only freed when all his wounds
speak to him. What the vine wants

happens. Stamping on the ground
makes little difference,
desperately little, to all around.

*

In the end I let you bathe in light
that rain is falling through.
If I turn round it might be

rainbowing. Around us is the

unspoken. By screwing the desk lamp
tighter to the windowsill,
I damage the inconstant
which I consist of. The hunt
of the null and void helps me
keep up disappearances better
than I will ever come to love.

*

Towards the end the cut withstands
the wound itself. Many of these worms
hope for recognition. The yielding

holds out a little longer.

A velvety tissue grows over

unjoyment, once most has been
seen through and wiped out. And so
it finally takes shape: a flake of
darkness, reborn through
insight into denying
this insight.

VI

from *Troublesome Gods*
(*Hinderlijke goden*)
1985

from *Self-Dispersing God*

*

The vase
I am holding in my hands
and carrying to the kitchen
to fill with water

lacks neither the vase
it is and will be, nor

the vase which a moment ago
bursts into flames once again,
and only then dashes itself
to pieces on the ground.

*

The notion that my body
hatches something that houses

my death – or that

in this it is only being itself,
putting itself to the test,
holding itself in check,
this body, already become
through me so dearly
devoted to itself.

'My love, the hart of time,

once sped hence,
never returns.'

Someone sees through his metaphor
700 years ago and ever after
is enacted again and again

by the metaphor itself;

or that yet another dolphin
takes someone like that on its back, holds
his head above water, carries him to shore
and only then pushes him over the edge.

*

The fragile, the disquieting
lies open and shows what has become
of itself under the sun, since then.

Behind my shoulders nothing remains;
I go up in flames. And yet in this
I can see I am lying. What use
is a millipede: first

I embraced myself, then let
myself be embraced as told
in the text: as if the father of
all croppers cannot leap clear
of a single leap forward.

from *Troublesome Gods*

*

This is how I goes under,
grows riddled and homeless

and has gone under; yet still
to this very day refuses

the arrant emptiness which
leaves even itself at a loss,
though all the gods were to blow
all the other gods through
the only gods remaining.

*

Shearing along
the blade –
just look at the swallows!

In order to be foiled
before it is too late, smoke,
continually postponed, weathers
all these worries, which may

even precede the bleeding dry
so as to need foiling
by fire, by smoke, and by
nothing else but fire
and smoke.

*

The muffled thud with which the strange cat
lands in the room, and wakes me.
While she carries on sleeping

I look at the cat. This cat knows
I'm seeing it. The same moonless
night that on Hadrian's Wall

a snowy owl is sitting, motionless:
until the cat suddenly begins
to lick itself all over and I must have
shifted position. Are you awake?
(Shssst.) Go away cat.

*

'Although I am a swallow
who wants to be a horse, and by
being a horse have first been

a swallow.' By whirling round
and round I turn into nothing. But

where are her nine books, where

is Corinna, where Anyte; where are
Orpheus, Archilochus, Alcaeus;
whatever happened to Alcman the slave.

I scrape my spit together, see
through all oblivion, lose my way,
act out a well, even ape
myself. What a relief. Nothing
helps; this is how it is.

from *Pierced*

for Salvador Hertog

Extremely slowly the snail
crosses the path, and before
she knows it she is saved.

But in the undergrowth,

where the leaves are,
where it is cool,
the consummation awaits her:
to be absorbed into a greater
whole, a drier, swifter creature.

*

What it is all about,
I repeat, is
next to nothing.

A tiny dun spider,
with a tinge of rust,
which I cautiously approach
with my forefinger, suddenly
jumps almost a meter
away from me.

*

The night is mortal;

the rowan has come to herself;
the chair is on the patio;
the water in the tap.

And then the sea, her rock. O

shelter, throbbing with farewell.

Its coming, nor going.
A spade, nor a swan.

*

It has been thundering;
and has let itself rain.

The web is no longer really intact.

I start wanting to tease the creature.
I've almost forgotten myself; and I hold myself
back. I see how majestically the spider
in her castle in the air keeps leaving undone

what I expect. Long before I
get through to me, I've started
feeling ashamed of myself.

*

One of my hands rises,
descends, and touches on something.
It is the time required.
It has come to a dead end.

The crucial is collected

and the water, in the wicker basket,
almost the divine, raised,
lets itself fall, is half-way down
the wall, looks over the wall
and has let itself fall.

I suddenly turn round.
It stays no longer hidden,

has wriggled free in me.

While I come closer I am

seen through. It is a flower
I do not know, which knew
me for who I am, carries me ashore,
gradually lays me down just like
the sea sometimes does with someone
who must have drowned.

I fill my lungs and enter
the inn, quivering with farewell.
I do what has been done.

The owl who guards the glassware here

has seen to everything. I have to
strain my ears to hear nothing
but the rushing I know. Pink
and white geraniums where the windows

were, water where the pump was,
memory what I was like, where I am.

*

If the opening were forever
pierced by the opened,
nothing would remain in the end
but the same, fanning out
till night strikes, declares that

enough is enough. If someone
should choose his death: whose
chosen one is he, through
whom does he shudder thither?

Love dons her black cap
and kills. Even an onion surrenders
all in the end. Just as a chair, in spite
of everything, everywhere and nowhere,
wishes only to sit in for itself.

*

Although is is forever
itself, it constantly has to
be summoned. To this end
I summon and I am summoned.

The work whose end I serve
must make headway;

if not – the grasses will wither,

the mountain collapse, the tent
it lives in blow away, water
begin to burn as far as the horizon,
till in the end reigns only absolute
memory of hissing perception,
forever self-voiding oblivion.

More fleeting than my shadow is,
the myrtle has no scent. No man
can manage to be more fragile
than the mortal inside me.

As soon as I am summoned, I come
into being in order to disappear.
Love serves the forgetting; the shirt
the wind has left behind will not

fit me. I usually have to
do what I want so that I
may die as befits me.

*

Everything existing stretches
to the edge of being, curls up,
casts out and recaptures itself –

until this being, having held itself

out to the end, compelled to do so

by a tempting motif, accepts its
is to be rising, and of its own accord,
while a person smiles to himself,
it reaches the edge and boils over,
a foaming deeply foaming
into the nothing I am.

VII

from *Against the Forgetting*
(*Tegen het vergeten*)
1988

from *Against the Forgetting*

*

To be able to lash out
at the same,

in vain:

is this not the privilege
a person claims,
assumes in order
to forget he remembers
how a red kite hove into view

over the wheatwood
and clawed him to a shrew.

*

As soon as I raise my eyes
the invisible has slipped away
and I begin to see what I see:
memories of what I have seen

and whatever I will see. By seeing
I keep remembering;

hoping that I exist.

Especially when I look at her
as she runs her hand like that
through her hair, her elbow
resting on her knee, and she
says something to me.

*

Why did she not stay where she is,
if she is not here and would rather
have gone there than be as one
with what remains when all

is destroyed: letting herself

slip onewards just as she is:
an almost beautiful beautiful woman
balancing on the edge of herself,
trying to convince me she exists

just because I'm lying in her arms

in which I've never been lying,
nor ever will, anyway.

*

Beating his lead with the blunt
end of his axe, flattening it
in order to forget that he is

a child of death who wants to weight

his net. Until it is suddenly done
and the undisappeared
stands in my room, taking me
in; still lying whether I am,

and how. Just as you might ask
a fisherman returning with nothing:
So where's the fish? And for him to reply,
without resentment, without envy:
The fish – it's in the sea.

from *How Forever Once*

As a woman might
give or not give herself,

in calculation, in love;
a maple leaf have long begun
its fall, or have not quite
let go its branch;

the drops of water on my lips
how mindful of their river still,
its flow – but no longer of
the sea of clouds, so self-enlacing
in their billows, so self-effacing.

*

There is not much else than here.
Ideas are much like memories;

and most ideas go up in smoke,
long before their trial by fire.

The thinglike in the fleeting is what
deceives. Even the most real
does not exist as it seems;

as when I rise and walk towards you
and lapse myself in the scent of all
that dark hair, a plume of smoke, an echo
of nothing else than this very ever, this never,
this then from before you existed.

*

Night escapes its shades of dawn,
as the moonlight still bears traces
of the whisper basalt consists of.

What is at hand, as far as it lends
sense, offers itself and stretches,

incessantly. The hart now said to be
on the run dissolves around the skyline
in ever more scents, which let it be known
why hawthorn blossom resists

its withering so. And while even
the most fleeting meanings are shaken
anew, eye, ear and voice strip
the darkness of all its delicate
glistening scales with brisk
little kitchen knives.

from *Sequence Against Death*

*

The eyes which grant
my eyes her eyes,
because this is how

the light in them goes between;

the bracken, once I, stepping out of the stream,
was walking up the slope and smelt the woods;
the sweet chestnuts in the basket,
in the print on the wall
by the balcony;

the stylish new shoes you will be
taking on your journey tomorrow.

Is the same not good enough then;
or does it hurt more really than then.

But what then is love;

and is it right to love,
and grip to the mortal.
And so to grip the helm;
to row upriver, against
the current, even if it doesn't

get me half a boat-length forward;
if the stubborn willows cannot help
doing what has to come to pass, in
the name and honor of their seasons.

*

Its only riddle: *how*
it is; how that leaves it

at a loss, at less
than a loss, for words.

That I'm standing straight among rising plants.
That what encircles me like a world
takes possession of me, just as
what I keep veiled like a mist
wants to be possessed

by me. Listen! as the stone
splits the stream, so the chestnut keeps
its shiny silence; the antlion will never
embrace its ant and help it out of the funnel,
back to its antlike freedom.

from *The Parapet*

How come the unmoving
is so within me in leaping
flame, in cooing stone,
your wafting wings, Erra.

The old man, busy crossing
to the shady side of the square:
do not snatch away his stick. The girl
waiting to bleed for the first time:

help her; do not smash, with a single
sweep of your arm, all the glasses
to the ground. Do not throw
stones at a stranger
in a blind alley.

I warn you: mind you
do not do this, Nergal, or
I will silence you dead.

*

The angel leans further and further
over the parapet, until
his wings start tingling
with excitement. Should he

hurl himself down, perhaps,
and give them a taste
of what an angel is made of?
Further and further:

the tingling, the longing
in his pinions; repeating
the spells, the spells forgotten;

delusion, or essence, or beyond
them both. So why isn't he
humming, that angel of yours,
that shadow already turning purple
where there used to be a parapet?

from *Persephone, Resurrected*

*

Time and again I have to love you,
for you are what is so utterly strange
to me; almost as strange to me

as my being's core, which is
a wingbeat still lasting
long after the memory

of my name has evaporated. Sometimes,
once I become aware of myself
and our house starts to rustle
and I am tempted to call out

your name, I find you in my head
again, as if I had not meant
to caress you, caress you so.

*

Spring, it must be. Persephone,

a little absent-mindedly still, opens
her satin peignoir, folds her hands
behind her head, breathes in deeply, holds

her breath a moment, and breathes out deeply,
deeply. Now, accustomed to the light,
she starts to see what she knew,
hardly perturbed by what she

knows must come. Her eyes are hazel,

her hair ashblonde, but her neck
has the scent of now and never.
Oh, kidlike it bounded forward,
and licked the milk from her shell.

VIII

from *Default*
(*Het ontbrokene*)
1990

from *Default*

On its ever so tricky thread
a tiny sovereign spider

descends into the abyss and edges
my body aside. It is a spider,

which delays its landing till I have
retired from its crevice. Once it has

touched bottom, this is the signal
that the river has stormed its source.

*

On a hiding to nothing
with these thoughts that now,

mindful of the ebony vault
surrounding their absence,

threaten more temptingly than ever
before, with an ever keener yearning

for their pilfered crystals,
to free themselves of me as the same.

*

Doesn't the shadowy rose
which I am shown in the depths

of the word death, smell
of trampled grapes, murdered for their

soul, which is also mine; your voice
of the skin, still warm, which the wind

let go and yielded up; violin resin
for an axe's tears, reviled?

*

Letting a night train
run your head from your body:

that took more courage than to keep
realizing how more and more leaks

out of the same about the same.
As soon as the whip releases its top,

as light pulls the sting of love,
night irresistibly falls.

*

Shortly before it is too late,
what was called beauty passes away

at least to the lightfall in the navel
of an old man, who, thinking he might

die, no longer took the trouble
to close his curtains. And yet

it remains the same river, which, delirious
with love, wishes, thinks, pierces, is.

*

Casting all caution aside,
the wind now drives its rutting waves

through wheat and rye, over
the stonefields, between the bayonets

of forgotten armies; till it loses
itself, pauses for breath, regroups

about that luminous opening,
to sealess distance in salt.

from *A Watering Can*

The way a man stands in his garden,
after the rain, in his old bleu-de-Nîmes
togs, straightens a few fallen
peonies; his short cough, which

makes the sun break briefly through;
forgetting, it seems, the motionless

granite sea beneath his feet,
risen from one of his thousand
deaths; a man in his garden,
a short-lived awning
over what is.

*

The train scarcely slackens speed
and he is there: much the same man.

Now he is standing beside his house:
a watering can at hand, his eyes
to the ground.

The ground around him is damp;
his desire is fled and gone. What he
does not wish to know, under any
circumstances, is where and when he will be
demanded back and claimed
by the ground around him.

*

She has let herself fall on her bed
just as she fell there. But now she is
no longer crying; her makeup has run,
drying gold-dust stains her cheek,
her hair is dishevelled.

On the folding screen which has no
more chances to get used to her,
a dragon is forever diving for its pearl,
Zeno's arrow is followed time and again
by another which splits it in two.

from *Four Poems and Rosamund*

*

Seldom has a panther's leap
anything at all of the same leap
by the same panther, unless as
willed by the panther itself.

The dolphin swimming in front of the ship
keeps swimming in front of the ship
until there is definitely no longer
a dolphin swimming in front of a ship.

And so it will come to pass that you scarcely notice

the sweat in your armpits changing smell,
that you fail to see the centaur scrape
his hooves before he advances towards you,
and here where you're safe at home
kicks and smashes it all to smithereens.

*

To stare without desire, with no
hope of reward, nor in fear of punishment,
at the reckless, the merciless beauty

where emptiness imparts itself,
expresses itself in what exists.

May the god who hides inside me be willing
to hear me, to let me speak out,
before he strikes me dumb and kills me
under my very eyes, under your very eyes.

IX

from *Spring Foxes*
(Springvossen)

2000

*

As simple as a drop of water,
as clear as a splinter of birch,

Because the foal falls patiently, cautiously
out of the horse and is able to stand,

And the fish unfolds like a metal tear
and is able to fly, and people quand même

Are slow to learn silence and absence
amidst their armored scree,

It isn't as simple, as clear
what I'm left with when I
have put down my pen.

*

Nowhere has denying
reigned as rife as in this not
which is outsitting me here.

Oh, if only death would
outstare itself for ever
in its iron mirror.

God, what a down-at-heel hope
for a voiceless evaporation

with wind and light as the silent
witnesses which one finds here.

Yesterday, yes, I still existed here:
in this pitiful winestain,
in these paupered words
way past their prime,

in that handshake which I
will never manage to hold
in any of my handbooks,

and which under my table leads
the still life of a retired
country doctor.

Go on, admit it:
yesterday you also existed here,

when the sun turned up humming
and we took in the fact that
neither one of us, in this circus,
dared fight
the bear.

*

With one hand in my lap,
with my other hand on the table.
My head is located above it;

in which a landscape drops anchor, sun-drenched.

It is one moonless evening.

While his son carefully

draws the sculls through the water,
his father stands by the hissing lamp,

leaning forward, peering into the sea,
trident raised. Where is it,
now that I am writing it; where am I,
now that you are re-reading this?

Since nobody was there anyway,
and since it's not blocked off,
it's time for a walk once again
along the brink of the beach, where all
of a sudden the woods held back,
or have withdrawn by degrees.

Thinking this is someone who does
not know that he is in this text
and will never get out again,
however he tinkers with sentences
and shifts the meanings about.

Better that than the other way round,
when cold strikes without warning;
and better never than late.
Here I go thinking this again.

In all my absence here
there lurks a triumph which
will never rest on its laurels.

One fine day it was night.
I seemed to be just
about to catch my first
fish. Suddenly it all

conspires against me.
It was too late
to unbait my hook.

I head for home,

humming in my sleep,
to worship the dark-
ness, with pounding heart.

*

If later, or sooner, it is,
or becomes, sayable – this is the most
thingable it will be; best of all,
let my text encircle someone

who foists it on himself,

or by whom it's fobbed off with itself;
if smoke fails to announce the outcome,
I might as well go to sea:
to let oneself be blown away.

*

'Then they went away too.'
Hardly had I known them.
I also hardly stayed behind.
I would have liked to write something
down, but I had forgotten to write

it down. If you listen

to people, it's all about a future
which lives in a pebble and is as smooth
as the self-same pebble. Now and again
I own such a pebble as well: a moment
before I've thrown it away.

Translator's Notes

6   *noise*: in the English in the original, thus with the specific sense of "white noise."

25   *Hercules Seghers*: Dutch artist (c.1589–c.1633). His engraving "View of Rhenen" inspired a cycle in *Lightfall*.

29   *The ruins . . .* is quoted from Hölderlin. *Not even a flea . . .* : cf. the Russian proverb "A flea cannot jump between life and death" (i.e. the boundary is indistinguishable).

30   *Now the hour is standing still*: in his poetry, Faverey rarely used images from his work as a clinical psychologist. Here, however, he mentioned that the poem was inspired by a paper about the electroencephalogram of a dying man.

58   *The thornback, pregnant . . .* : at the quayside on the Dalmatian island of Šipan, where Hans and Lela used to spend their summers, they once saw a fisherman who had landed a pregnant thornback – a flatfish that bears live young. A friend carefully slit its belly open and eased the tiny fish back into the sea, at which they swam away.

62   A German friend once told Faverey about a visit to a fair as a child. Seeing a tent entitled *Das Jenseits* (The Other Side), she bought a ticket and took her place in the audience. Finally the curtain opened – to reveal the other side of the river by which the fair was held.

63   Many of Faverey's poems are set in or allude to landscapes and people from the Dalmatian islands and inland Croatia, especially Slavonia. Here, Hans and Lela are standing in her aunt's garden in Nova Gradiška.

66   *Bite the dust*: in the original, *ondergaan* ("go under," i.e. "come to grief").

67   *Oblivion knows no time*: *Vergetelheid kent geen tijd* reminds the Dutch reader of the proverb *Gezelligheid kent geen tijd* – i.e. time flies when you're enjoying yourself.

71   *Girolamo Cavazzoni*: Italian composer (c.1510–c.1580). Hans Faverey played the harpsichord.

72 *cancel one another out*: the Dutch *wegvallen tegen elkaar* (literally "fall away against one another") mirrors "falling back once more" later in the poem.

75 *ex improviso*: a term in organ music. "The keyboard" is that of the harpsichord.

85 *If I so much as move a muscle / I have to admit I'm // a shellfish.*: the Dutch for "move a muscle" is "move a fin." Hence, in Faverey's original, he then has to admit he is a fish.

90 Hans Faverey was born in Dutch Guiana (now Surinam), and his father died there. "Spider" is Anansi of the West Indian folk tales. The verb-form "You going ... " is intended to give the Caribbean flavor of *je gaat ...*: Netherlands Dutch prefers to construct its future tense with *je zult ...* ("you shall").

98 The whole poem is riddled with double meanings, making it more difficult to translate than most. "Only then is there sense ... " tries to convey the double meaning of *zin* (sense/sentence) by means of expansion; a literal translation would be "Only then is it time to strip the sense/sentence of all its words."

102 *Ningal*: in the Assyrian Epic of Gilgamesh, the wife of the Moon God and the mother of the Sun.

104 Cf. note to page 63. The Croatian for "reeds" is *šaš*, pronounced "shash."

120 *her nine books*: Sappho's.
     Corinna, Anyte, Archilochus, Alcaeus, Alcman: ancient Greek poets.

128 *to sit in for itself*: the Dutch *bezeten* means both "sat upon" and "possessed" – here, in the daemonic sense.

145 *Nergal*: the Assyrian god of plague and of the underworld.

INDEX OF FIRST LINES

New Directions Paperbooks—A Partial Listing

For a complete listing request free catalog from New Directions, 80 Eighth Avenue, New York 10011; or visit our website, www.ndpublishing.com

†Bilingual

Forrest Gander, *Torn Awake.* NDP926.
Romain Gary, *The Life Before Us,* NDP604.
William Gerhardie, *Futility.* NDP722.
Goethe, *Faust (Part I).* NDP70.
Henry Green, *Pack My Bag.* NDP984.
Allen Grossman, *Sweet Youth.* NDP947.
Martin Grzimek, *Heartstop.* NDP583.
Henri Guigonnat, *Daemon in Lithuania.* NDP592.
Lars Gustafsson, *The Tale of a Dog.* NDP868.
Sam Hamill, *The Infinite Moment.* NDP586.
Knut Hamsun, *Dreamers.* NDP821.
John Hawkes, *The Beetle Leg.* NDP239.
   The Blood Oranges. NDP338.
   Death, Sleep, and the Traveler. NDP393..
Samuel Hazo, *Thank A Bored Angel.* NDP555.
Robert E. Helbling, *Heinrich von Kleist.* NDP390.
William Herrick, *That's Life.* NDP596.
Hermann Hesse, *Siddhartha.* NDP65.
Yoel Hoffmann, *Katschen & The Book of Joseph.*
   NDP875.
   The Shunra and the Schmetterling. NDP980.
Paul Hoover, *The Novel.* NDP706.
Susan Howe, *The Midnight.* NDP956.
   Pierce-Arrow. NDP878.
Hsieh Ling-Yün, *The Mountain Poems.* ND928.
Vicente Huidobro, *The Selected Poetry.* NDP520.
Qurratulain Hyder, *River of Fire.* NDP952.
Christopher Isherwood, *All the Conspirators.*
   NDP480.
   The Berlin Stories. NDP134.
Philippe Jaccottet, *Seedtime.* NDP428.
Fleur Jaeggy, *SS Proleterka.* NDP758.
   Sweet Days of Discipline. NDP758.
Henry James, *The Sacred Fount.* NDP790.
Gustav Janouch, *Conversations with Kafka.* NDP313.
Alfred Jarry, *Ubu Roi.* NDP105.
Robinson Jeffers, *Cawdor and Medea.* NDP293.
B.S. Johnson, *Albert Angelo.* NDP628.
   House Mother Normal. NDP617.
Gabriel Josipovici, *In a Hotel Garden.* NDP801.
James Joyce, *Finnegans Wake: A Symposium.*
   NDP331.
   Stephen Hero. NDP133.
Franz Kafka, *Amerika: The Man Who Disappeared.*
   NDP981.
Bilge Karasu, *The Garden of the Departed Cats.*
   NDP965.
Mary Karr, *The Devil's Tour.* NDP768.
Bob Kaufman, *The Ancient Rain.* NDP514.
John Keene, *Annotations.* NDP809.
Heinrich von Kleist, *Prince Friedrich of Homburg.*
   NDP462.
Kono Taeko, *Toddler-Hunting.* NDP867.
Deszö Kosztolányi, *Anna Édes.* NDP772.
László Krasznahorkai, *The Melancholy of Resistance.*
   NDP936.
Rüdiger Kremer, *The Color of the Snow.* NDP743.
Miroslav Krleža, *On the Edge of Reason.* NDP810.
Shimpei Kusano, *Asking Myself/Answering Myself.*
   NDP566.
Davide Lajolo, *An Absurd Vice.* NDP545.

P. Lal, ed., *Great Sanskrit Plays.* NDP142.
Tommaso Landolfi, *Gogol's Wife.* NDP155.
James Laughlin, *The Love Poems,* NDP865.
   Poems New and Selected. NDP857.
Comte de Lautréamont, *Maldoror.* NDP207.
D.H. Lawrence, *Quetzalcoatl.* NDP864.
Irving Layton, *Selected Poems.* NDP431.
Christine Lehner, *Expecting.* NDP572.
Siegfried Lenz, *The German Lesson.* NDP618.
Denise Levertov, *The Life Around Us.* NDP843.
   Selected Poems. NDP968.
   The Stream and the Sapphire. NDP844.
   This Great Unknowing. NDP910.
Li Ch'ing-Chao, *Complete Poems.* NDP492.
Li Po, *The Selected Poems.* NDP823.
Enrique Lihn, *The Dark Room.*† NDP452.
Clarice Lispector, *The Hour of the Star.* NDP733.
   Near to the Wild Heart. NDP698.
   Soulstorm. NDP671.
Luljeta Lleshanaku, *Fresco.* NDP941.
Federico García Lorca, *The Cricket Sings.*† NDP506.
   Five Plays. NDP506.
   In Search of Duende.† NDP858.
   Selected Letters. NDP557.
   Selected Poems.† NDP114.
Xavier de Maistre, *Voyage Around My Room.*
   NDP791.
Stéphane Mallarmé, *Mallarmé in Prose.* NDP904.
   Selected Poetry and Prose.† NDP529.
Oscar Mandel, *The Book of Elaborations.* NDP643.
Abby Mann, *Judgment at Nuremberg.* NDP950.
Javier Marías, *All Souls.* NDP905.
   A Heart So White. NDP937.
   Tomorrow in the Battle Think On Me. NDP923.
Bernadette Mayer, *A Bernadette Mayer Reader.*
   NDP739.
Michael McClure, *Rain Mirror.* NDP887.
Carson McCullers, *The Member of the Wedding.*
   NDP394.
Thomas Merton, *Bread in the Wilderness.* NDP840.
   Gandhi on Non-Violence. NDP197.
   New Seeds of Contemplation. NDP337.
   Thoughts on the East. NDP802.
Henri Michaux, *Ideograms in China.* NDP929.
   Selected Writings.† NDP263.
Henry Miller, *The Air-Conditioned Nightmare.*
   NDP587.
   The Henry Miller Reader. NDP269.
   Into the Heart of Life. NDP728.
Yukio Mishima, *Confessions of a Mask.* NDP253.
   Death in Midsummer. NDP215.
Frédéric Mistral, *The Memoirs.* NDP632.
Eugenio Montale, *Selected Poems.*† NDP193.
Paul Morand, *Fancy Goods* (tr. by Ezra Pound).
   NDP567.
Vladimir Nabokov, *Laughter in the Dark.* NDP729.
   Nikolai Gogol. NDP78.
   The Real Life of Sebastian Knight. NDP432.
Pablo Neruda, *The Captain's Verses.*† NDP345.
   Residence on Earth,† NDP340.
Robert Nichols, *Arrival.* NDP437.

For a complete listing request free catalog from New Directions, 80 Eighth
Avenue New York 10011; or go visit our website, www.ndpublishing.com

For a complete listing request free catalog from New Directions, 80 Eighth
Avenue, New York 10011; or visit our website, www.ndpublishing.com

†Bilingual